Many professional bettors, those who manage to earn through betting, argue that without effective technological help it is impossible to win very often. Instead, with a good dose of constancy and various attempts you can find a formula with which you can win often.

The goal of our guide is to try to help our bettors to develop a valid method to try to win with their bets in a simple and fast way

The first useful tip could be to not only play the main leagues, but look for low odds within minor leagues. Why is this? Because the average level of the teams that take part in these leagues is very low and the best teams manage to win a large amount of games.

At this point, you will have to enter about 3 or 4 of these events and hope! You will have, thus, a mix of bets between better and non-best leagues.

REMEMBER, ALWAYS PLAY CAREFULLY AND SPARINGLY. DON'T PLAY MORE THAN YOU CAN
LOSING EVERYTHING IS A MOMENT

A second piece of advice concerns, then, the type of odds to play. If you do not trust the 1X2 much on some games, you could consider the idea of playing some odds such as the over 1.5 or, alternatively, the under 3.5.

In some leagues, these odds are really very attractive and, for this reason, it will be sufficient to choose the right leagues and the right type of bet, betting the most suitable odds to have ready bets more income.

In addition, attention must be paid to bonuses, in fact most AAMS bookmakers provide their players with different types of betting bonuses. There are multiple bet bonuses, football betting bonuses or simply welcome bonuses, bonuses that are paid by the gaming portal when the player has completed the registration process.

In this sense, choosing a bookmaker turns out to be advantageous for the player, because it allows him to take advantage of interesting bonuses and promotions.

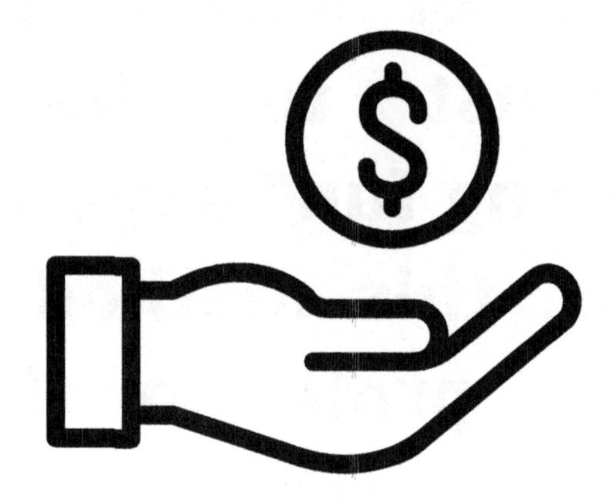

HERE ARE SOME GAMING SYSTEMS

This method is based on the statistics of goals scored in the first and second half, and consists of two or more bets, one in contrast to the other. "Having fun" a bit with the odds, this method pays a small profit in the vast majority of games.

In practice we will have to find that share that allows us to earn a minimum profit even with the loss of 1 or 2 results. Playing 3 spins only for a time the chances of going into profit are greater

Remember, you must always go with caution: to understand what is the right way to win, you have to experiment, test and then also lose (but respecting your budget, without haste to recover in the case, the lost money). You have to test many times and bang your head over and over again on many strategies and techniques.

It is necessary to do tests on tests to understand your most suitable strategy, using symbolic figures and doing simulations, research etc., writing everything in a notebook as it was once done

Remember, indicatively the lower the odds, the higher the chances of winning but having low profits.

The point is whether you want to win little but frequently or risk not winning almost never but when it happens to break the bank.

If you are at the beginning of your betting adventure I recommend 5 or 6 games to play

in a single ticket with a low score and increase your confidence with small but continuous winnings.

THE SINGLE

The advantage of playing single, as you well know, is to increase the share of events on the ticket and multiply the probability of success, because the odds are higher and compared to options such as over or under or odd and even. Obviously, the chances of success of individual matches are more difficult!

That's why it's only better to play single bets with high odds if you want to break through.

In doubles, on the other hand, the advantage is to increase the chances of our ready tickets. Why do we often opt for the double? Because the double is a compromise that allows you to choose with a limited number of events to bet and reduce the risk of the single prediction.

I recommend combining two low odds, which multiplied together give us a share equal to that of a single one in our opinion more risky.

The doubling method can be a good method but you have to choose the matches carefully. Calculate an amount between 12 and 15 euros. I recommend simple and not too risky matches, 3/4 games. You have to choose the amount of the initial bet, for example 3 or 5 euros. Then we select 2 tickets, one with our bet and the second with different results but with the same teams.

Finally, at the end of the first half, checking the games, we can decide whether to play another bet following the progress of the matches. In this way we could straighten out the trend of previous bets

REMEMBER, ALWAYS PLAY CAREFULLY AND SPARINGLY. DON'T PLAY MORE THAN YOU CAN

Another technique is the one that develops in six bets, the first is bet 1 euro on a game with a low odds. In case of winning, you play the win on a ticket with 2 games and so on until you lose. If you lose to start over with 1 game. The system is recommended for low odds, since to have a profit requires a series of winnings.

I recommend odds between 1.05 and 1.45 that guarantee a good success rate.

EVEN AND ODD

Technique for those who do not like to risk on exact results or are not good at predictions.
Play a bet slip with 4/5 games in which you bet only even or odd as you prefer. Then make 4 more slips reversing the various possibilities always betting even or odd.

Choose games with odds around 1.30/1.50. In this way in case of losses on the first / second attempt you should recover then going forward. I recommend bets around 2/3 euros. The fewer games played, obviously the higher the chances of winning, but the lower the profits.

Another system consists in playing one or more fixed with minimum total odds 2.00 and betting together the same game with 3 different results, namely EVEN, OVER and NO GOAL. In this case all the results would be covered and there are chances to take 2 results. In theory, the minimum payout will always be greater than the total bet. You have to play the odds of the OVER and NO GOAL that are around 2.00.

Among the bets and winning systems described, this is certainly one of the safest. Obviously, with this we cannot guarantee that you will go to the cashier because much depends on your ability to locate the fixed.

Another technique is to play 3/4 games with only one result, x or 1 sign in case of predictions in favor of the home team. A ticket always choosing the same teams with over and under 3.5 and the last ticket betting double results. Raise the odds to play with the bet with less profit.

REMEMBER, ALWAYS PLAY CAREFULLY AND SPARINGLY.
DON'T PLAY MORE THAN YOU CAN
LOSING EVERYTHING IS A MOMENT

One of the best-known methods is the integral system. This is a particular play, which is perhaps easier to play than to explain. It is enough to place multiple predictions, on a given sporting event, in such a way as to develop multiples. In this way, bettors can bet on different outcomes of the same event, increasing the chances of winning.

Bet around 2/3 euros to start. Based on the results, you decide how much to play, always without exaggerating.
But that's not all, I recommend 2 tickets of this type before the chosen games and 2 tickets always the same match but with different multiples.

One of the tactics that can be useful for winning sports bets is to mix together with other tactics that of referring to exact results or single plays. You can choose exact results or 2 hypothetical single plays of 1 or 2 certain matches of the tickets used with tactics seen above, and combine them together with other matches.

Remember, especially on the internet, we can find many (alleged) winning methods for betting. There is no real way that tells if a certain system is winning or not, but you can try a method and understand if it can meet our needs. Of course it takes perseverance and being able to stop and change when we go further.

REMEMBER, ALWAYS PLAY CAREFULLY AND SPARINGLY. DON'T PLAY MORE THAN YOU CAN

You can use the odd or even technique also with the odds of the goal and no goal, or mix these two techniques. Play 2 bets per tactic and a fifth with doubles, the recommended bugdet is 2 euros per ticket, in total you would play 10 euros but the chances of going into profit are good.

ODD METHOD + GOAL under 3.5 is a simple and easy to apply system, you have to choose 3/4 games, for example you could choose games that come from 5-6 evens in a row. So bet odds with odd and odds with under 3.5 Even if one of the two games ends 0-0 or 1-0 or 1-1 or 2-0 or 2-1 or 3-0 we have already won. So we have 6 chances to win.

Another technique is that of the over 0.5 in the first half and overlap a single live bet of betting games with this technique.
I would try with a bet of 5 games with over 0.5 and 2 single bets at the end of the first half on 2 same games played.
You can initially test various game tactics even in a notebook and from time to time write down the most prolific ones.

Progressive technique

It consists of playing for each bet made from time to time an extra euro in case of victory, continuing to increase the profit in case of a series of positive results and decrease by one euro at a time in case of lost bets.
In this way you should find yourself in profit over time.

Remember it is difficult to bet, win and change your life. In fact, it is almost impossible. However, you can play to have fun without squandering money and with a little luck and perseverance have small profits to take away some whim.

REMEMBER, ALWAYS PLAY CAREFULLY AND SPARINGLY. DON'T PLAY MORE THAN YOU CAN

Over 1.5, over 2.5 system, is a fun way and used by novice bettors. It is an easy system to follow with the progress of the various results. The system consists of choosing games that in our opinion have a high probability of ending up with Over 2.5. And cover the game with Over 1.5, creating a multiple system.

So we have to choose after a careful analysis of the matches, 4 games among those with a high probability of finishing over 2 goals. And select the bets of Over 2.5 and Over 1.5, so you create 16 tickets.
With an investment of € 2 of which € 0.25 per ticket, the minimum that can be played in most retailers you can earn between € 10-15 depends a lot on the odds.

Obviously, if you double the investment, the gain also doubles and we easily reach € 25 – € 50. The secret is to find games that have a high probability of ending up with many goals, but with a high odds.

Another very popular technique is to bet at the last minutes of a game maybe those that keep us more on our toes because the result could be completely overturned. I recommend with this technique to try once a month combined with some other ticket, I would stay on 5 euros initially. Let's see together how and what strategy to use towards the end of the game.

The first type of bet to consider is the "Over/Under" one. It's about betting on how many goals we think will be scored towards the end of the game, whether they are, "Under" or "Over" a certain number.

For example, in the last 20 minutes of play, you may decide to bet by establishing that more than two goals will be scored before the game ends.

If you study the various European leagues and we can not notice that some of them are more prolific in terms of goals from 70 minutes onwards.
If you can have a continuous winning streak you might think about increasing your budget.

Another option is to predict which of the two teams that are playing will score a goal first, whether it is a win or a draw. To make a prediction as plausible as possible, it is recommended to watch the match live to understand the course that the match is taking and thus make your choices.

I initially suggest to subscribe to more betting sites to have more bonuses to use, many sites to attract more customers offer entry bonuses that you can take advantage of to try more tactics and understand which technique is right for you.
Define your own budget to use and divide them among the various sites that offer you more bonuses, in this way you should already earn even before betting.

Another very useful strategy for goal bets at the end of the game is to compare and find bets with the highest odds, so that you can earn more. So as to find the most convenient share for a higher profit.

These techniques are just some of the tactics you can follow or try, but you can also mix these methods together or try various ways to find your own line of play.
Never risk more than you can and when you have a line of negative results stop and try to figure out if it's for you. Don't always gamble profits in the hope of earning more and more.

I recommend getting two small boxes, in one you deposit the money you want to bet in a month and in the other that of profits. Never mix the 2 boxes and after a few months you come to terms with the results obtained.

Printed in Great Britain
by Amazon

59658326R00030